CW01310816

EverydayCombat

Created & illustrated by

Thomas Corkett

EverydayCombat

This book has been created to help guide, educate and give you the tools on how to live the best possible life, being strong, resilient and happy in both mind and body.

Contents

Introduction - 9 - 12

Part I - Mental Fitness - 14 - 53

Confidence - 17 - 19

Failure - 20 - 23

Live Right - 24 - 29

Stop Worrying - 30 - 36

Love Yourself - 37 - 40

Control - 41 - 47

Pain - 48 - 51

No - 52 - 53

Part II - Habits - 55 - 74

Habit Creation - 59 - 65

Habit Breaking - 66 - 67

Good - 68 - 69

Bad - 70

Ugly - 71 - 72

Routine - 73 - 74

Part III - Be Dangerous - 76 - 96

Workout - 78 - 82

Mean It - 83 - 86

Don't Give A F*ck - 87 - 89

Create - 90 - 92

Stance - 93 - 96

Part IV - Wellness - 98 - 117

Emotional - 100 - 102

Spiritual - 103 - 104

Intellectual - 105 - 107

Social - 108 - 110

Physical - 111 - 113

Career - 114 - 117

Part V - EverydayCombat - 119 - 135

Pace - 121 - 122

Embrace - 123 - 125

Pressure - 126 - 127

Process - 128 - 129

Thrive - 130 - 132

Strive - 133 - 134

Succeed - 135

End notes - 137 - 142

Introduction

Having worked in the health and fitness industry for a number of years, both elements have always played a huge part in my life, whether it be professional or personal.

I've worked with, and have come across, a wide variety of individuals, from people with mental illness, others with more visible illnesses, and individuals living with terminal illnesses. I myself have also achieved and overcome multiple physically and mentally challenging experiences.

Having experienced this, I decided to look into the mental health, mental strength/fitness and illness side in more depth and have since become qualified in exercise for mental illness, along with many other mental health qualifications. I also practice strong mental resilience myself.

I did this because I have experienced first-hand that fitness isn't the be all and end all.

But the mind is.

Granted, everyone and their gran claim to be mental health professionals and to be ambassadors of mental health.

Yes, it's great so many people are aware of the importance of mental health. But this isn't a mental health book.

This book is about combating mental health by forging mental fitness and developing healthy daily habits to make you the most resilient and dangerous person you can possibly be to achieve and overcome anything life throws at you.

The idea of this book is to equip you for everyday life, to thrive every day and live the best possible life.

For every day we do combat with ourselves and our mind, so sharpen your mind and practice living right.

Throughout this book I will be sharing snippets of my experiences and also the knowledge I have picked up over the years to help and guide you on your journey to achieving a stronger more resilient mind and body.

Sometimes your old life has to fall apart before your new life can fall together. So don't hesitate to leave the past in the past and move forward.

This book will be the light leading the way.

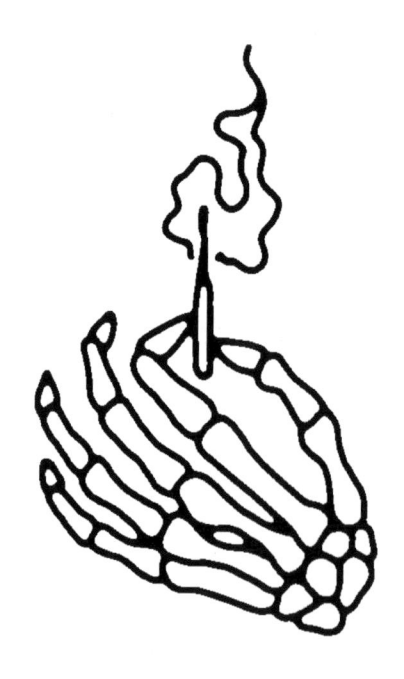

Part

I

Mental Fitness

Mental Fitness

What is mental fitness I hear you say. Well, simply put it's a combination of many attributes and daily actions which, when performed day in day as part of your daily routine, will help you develop mental fitness. This will help you overcome and achieve many things in your life, from the good to the bad.

Mental fitness is a relatively new phrase, it can be adapted to suit you and your own needs. But it's all about developing and forging a strong resilient mindset and body.

You may find you have a few of the traits we will cover over the coming pages but I'm sure there will be some that need work.

We are all a work in progress.

Mental health first, everything else will follow. The key to a healthy life is a healthy, strong, resilient mind.

Looking after yourself is not selfish, it's essential to your survival, well-being and mental fitness.

Make your mind and body bulletproof.

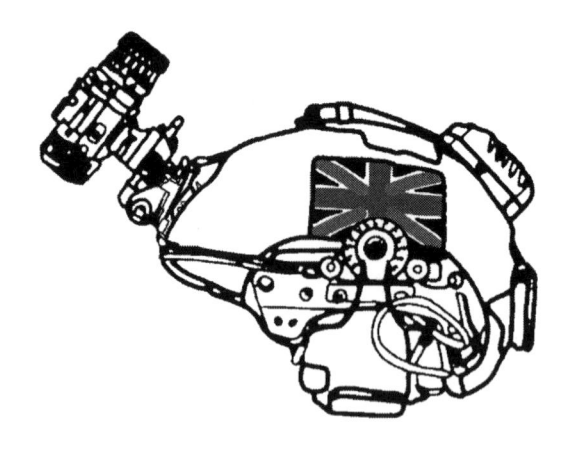

Confidence

Many of us seem to have it or act like we've got it, but in truth those who seem the most confident in their appearance are usually the least confident or lack confidence in other aspects of life.

Anyone can act confident, but it's our attitudes and approach to life that makes us truly confident.

True confidence is in yourself. Only you can give yourself true confidence. Don't rely on outside sources, people saying your selfie looks good, this is just praise.

Someone can dress up or pose in a mirror flexing, be loud, stand tall. But this isn't confidence, this is vanity and usually showing off.

Confidence and arrogance are different don't get them mixed up.

Don't rely on others, they can build it just as easily as they can destroy it.

It's all up to you. It can't be achieved over night; it's not achieved by a quick fix. But if you put in the work and practice you will achieve true confidence. But you have to be willing to work bloody hard.

So, how do we build confidence?

Firstly, I must iterate it's all up to you. Don't rely on others. They can big you up and make you feel good. This is praise, we all like praise but in the long run it's just bollocks and usually people blowing smoke up your arse. Take it with a pinch of salt, they probably want something.

You need to find out what you're capable of, or not in some cases. Building confidence is a slow process. One tiny step at a time. With the occasional step backwards. Don't let this put you off.

Put yourself in situations or positions which will expose your weaknesses, fears, emotions and insecurities, and do this time and time again.

Expose all of these, learn from them, and learn about them. The more you know about yourself the more your confidence will develop.

For example, say like me you're shit at exams, it usually takes me a couple of times to pass, whether it was my driving theory or my anatomy exams. When I was younger, I'd go in with an attitude of "I'll fail", and this attitude meant I did fail. Did it mean I was a bad driver or didn't know the difference between a toe and a finger.

No, it bloody didn't.

As soon as I realised this, I stopped being scared of going into exams or even avoiding them all together. I faced them head on, I put the work in before and went in with the attitude of "I will smash this". Yes, I still failed things. But it didn't stop or slow down my development like it did before.

Moral of the story, don't be scared to expose and show your weaknesses, fears, emotions and insecurities. The more you do it the more your confidence will increase.

Stick with it, there will be times it's very difficult but don't run and hide. One step at a time and face it head on.

Failure

This word scares the shit out of many people, they feel failure is the end and that's it for them. They are done.

This is absolute bollocks.

Failure is the biggest and best lesson we will ever learn. Turn failures into successes.

You only ever truly fail if you completely give up.

Embrace failure, as mentioned previously when building confidence, we must fail to reveal and find our true self. It is the only way we can truly learn about ourselves.

Building confidence and failure go hand in hand.

Failure is, and will always be, the best lesson we will ever get. Accepting and learning from these lessons will allow us to learn and grow more than you will ever know or realise at the time. In the moment some failures could feel like the end of the world and like you want to run away and hide. But give it time and every failure, no matter how big or small, will be a lesson that has allowed us to learn and grow.

Failure is on you, no one else. If you like to point the finger and believe you're never in the wrong, get a hold of yourself. We're human, we all fuck up, it's in our nature. Accept you've failed, hold your hands up and say yes, I fucked up, but what's the lesson or lessons I'll take away from this.

Blaming others doesn't only make you look an absolute dick, but it also deprives you of any lessons the failure would teach you. So it then becomes an almighty cluster fuck.

Don't point fingers or pass the blame. Have the balls to say it was you, your later self will thank you for it.

Failures aren't final nor are they fatal, not learning from them is. Don't live in the past, it's done, it's been, nothing you can do about it now. Don't dwell, don't let it control your future or hold you back.

What's happened in your past doesn't matter, what does matter is how you react and respond. This is what people will see and remember.

Don't bury your head.

Failures are obstacles, obstacles don't block the path. They are the path.

Live Right

Living right is all down to leading a healthy balanced lifestyle, there are many layers to doing this.

Simply put it's all down to routine and habits. The right habits.

If you've a good daily routine in place you will thrive. We need structure to do this.

Granted, sometimes the shit hits the fan and even the best laid plans go tits up. But, even when this happens, everything preceding and proceeding it are routine. Sometimes going a little off track isn't all bad, it adds a bit of variety.

When I say routine, I don't mean:

0600 **Wake up**

0630-0715 **This**

0730 **That**

0800 **Walk the dog**

0930 **Stuff**

And so on...

Yes, this could help some individuals that really need their hand holding. But if it is this structured, things will inevitably go tits up. There's too much to go wrong. It's to set in stone.

Then when things do go wrong you flap and the whole day goes to shit. When in truth it's nothing mega.

Make it simpler and more achievable.

Say you want to make sure you get to the gym; this can be done anytime around other tasks.

Each and every day is different. Some days you may have the kids, other days work may over run or maybe you're ill or just not feeling 100%.

Set an alarm to wake up and set a bedtime and mealtimes, you need to eat and drink. But what you do around these times will vary. Give yourself a list of tasks you want to do; gym, get fresh air, walk the dog, meditate etc...

Tick these off throughout the day.

Celebrate the small victories.

Make the most out of every day and be sensible with your routine.

Never go after quick fixes, we see everywhere these fat loss pills, shakes, wraps, potions or whatever bullshit people are selling or promoting. Or 7-day abs and other bollocks these wannabe fitness influencers promote.

Quick fixes aren't a lifestyle, they are exactly what they say on the tin, a quick fix.

Short term fine, if you have a beach holiday in 2 weeks that you need to look half decent for. But what about feeling and looking good every day for the rest of your life, not just for a few days on a beach.

There are many habits that create and forge a healthy, balanced and maintainable lifestyle. More of which will be covered in later pages.

Living right is a combination of many things.

Eat right and drink enough water. Eating right isn't brain surgery.

We all know what foods are right for us and what portions we should have on our plate. If you eat right, you will see the difference.

I hate the word diet; we all need to be more nutritionally aware. This is eating the right foods and nutrients and in the correct portions. Eating too little is just as bad as eating too much.

Simply put, you eat shit you'll feel like shit.

And water; it's pretty simple.

Drink or die.

Remember the rule of 3:

3 minutes without oxygen

3 days without water

3 weeks without food

Remember to breath.

Stop Worrying

I've said it countless times to people, stop worrying, don't worry, nothing to worry about...

Easier said than done right?

Many of us get wrapped up in the past and future and forget to live in the present.

We can't predict the future or change what has passed. So why dwell and waste our time, thoughts, and sanity on doing so.

Live in the moment.

Many of us live in a world of "what if", this needs to stop. If all we ever did was sit and say "what if I did that, what if I said that, what if, what if..." you're wasting your life.

You can't change it. As mentioned previously, learn from it.

The future is a mystery, accept it.

We don't have a crystal ball to tell us what's going to happen to us tomorrow, next week or even next year. We need to embrace it, accept it, and not worry about it.

Whatever happens, happens.

Deal with it when it happens.

If you worry about it, you're only putting yourself through it more times than is necessary.

Learn to control what's in your power and say fuck it to what isn't.

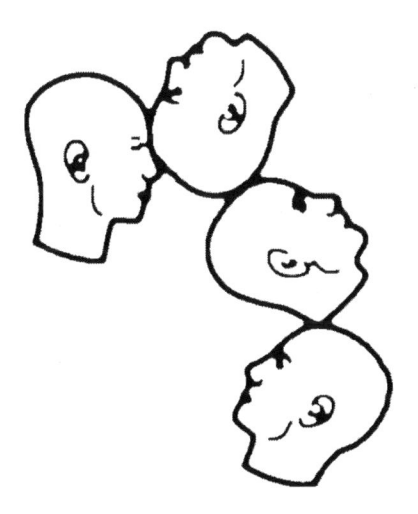

This is called stoicism; the stoics can teach us a great deal of how to live our lives.

One of their most known sayings is Amor Fati

This may be translated as "love of fate" or "love of one's fate".

It is used to describe an attitude in which one sees everything that happens in one's life, including suffering and loss, as good or, at the very least, necessary.

We've all been told everything happens for a reason. At the time we all go "shit reason" or "bollocks". But it's true. So many times, bad situations and moments have led me to bigger and better things.

So, don't worry. What happens will always happen.

Accept, embrace, learn and move forward. Worrying will weigh you down, most of the time we worry more than is necessary.

Nothing lasts forever, think of the long term. What you're worrying about now will soon be a distant memory and you'll be calling yourself an idiot for worrying about it. See the future as bright and full of opportunities for you.

If you constantly worry you will feel the future is dangerous and will only bring troubled times and disappointment. But, in fact it will most likely bring the opposite, it's not all doom and gloom. There is always light at the end of the tunnel, always.

When we worry, we create anxiety, this is crippling to us. It's like building a brick wall around ourselves, with our own thoughts, it's hard to escape and with each thought we add another brick.

But we can turn this anxiety into a positive. Hard to believe I know, but it is possible.

If you're worried you won't pass the exam you've got coming up, use the worry and anxiety to motivate you and drive you to revise more.

We suffer more in imagination than we do in reality.

Gym anxiety is rife. If someone is judging or looking don't take it personally. Too many people worry about this and don't go the gym at all.

It cripples you; it stops you doing what you need to do.

Many of us worry about finances and money, we always want more. The more we have the more we want. Money isn't the be all and end all.

Money can't buy you: Manners, Morals, Respect, Character, Common sense, Trust, Patience, Class, Integrity, Love.

Value your time more than your possessions.

Too many people are obsessed over money and are materialistic and show of their lives on social media. We see this and worry that we are failing.

Don't worry about this, not all things are as good as they look.

Turn a negative into a positive.

Turn worry into action.

Fuck the past.

Love Yourself

Resist the urge and pressure to look like someone else.

Easier said than done, especially with social media.

Stop treating social media like a shop, you want those legs, these arms, that arse.

Social media has a lot to answer for. We look online and we are bombarded by images of individuals who have had a lot of work done and are skilled at photo-shop and using filters.

These aren't realistic images, but we still look and want to be like them.

Remember:

You can't polish a shit, but you can roll it in glitter

Loving yourself doesn't mean you need to be arrogant.

It means you accept who you are and you're happy in your own skin, you love who you are inside and out.

We are all unique in our own way, celebrate these differences and embrace them.

Some of us are born with differences, some of us have them thrust upon us and some of us choose to make differences to ourselves.

Unfortunately, the latter is usually performed because we see people online who have perfect skin, bigger tits, bigger arse or bigger lips. This isn't healthy, embrace what you have and love you for who you are.

Granted I'm covered in tattoos, as are many of my friends. These are my choice. I love them and the artistry involved, plus they tell my story. I don't get them to please others or to look like anyone else.

No one has the perfect body, simple. We all have parts of ourselves we dislike.

Some things we can change, some things we can't. Accept it.

There's no cosmetic enhancement that can improve your physical and mental health, only your image.

Never be ashamed of looking after yourself, it's not vain or selfish. It's looking after yourself. Do whatever you want to look after yourself, go to spas, get haircuts, go to the gym.

Do what you want but do it for you and only you. Fuck what anyone else does and never do it for their benefit, only for yours.

Stop seeking external validation, social media has made us believe that this is the only way to achieve happiness.

Likes don't equal happiness.

Even the prettiest of things have demons within.

How can we love others if we don't truly love ourselves first.

Negative self-talk is the fastest way to tear down your mental toughness. So, don't. Speak only of yourself positively, be your own biggest supporter.

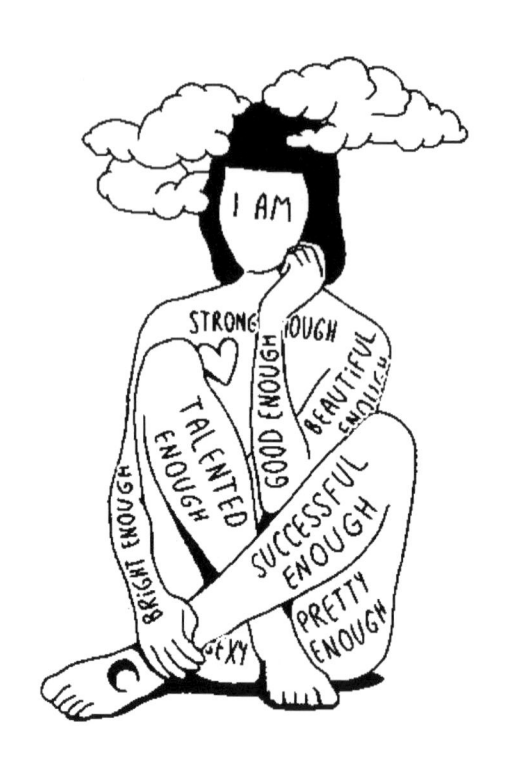

Control

Be in control of your emotions, don't let them control you.

As soon as you let your emotions take control you lose yourself. There is no harm or weakness in showing emotion, but you decide when you do it and how you do it.

I've experienced multiple different ways people release their emotions, some good, some bad.

I'll be the first to admit I used to be the latter, the emotion I used to show was anger. If something upset or angered me then I would get angry, not with other people but with myself. I would take it out on objects, hard objects such as walls or road signs, I would hit them, and I'd hit them hard. I remember being told my late dog (Jonah) had cancer, I got off the phone and continuously laid into a wall, breaking multiple bones in my hand.

Straight afterwards I was like "you fucking idiot". I let my emotions control me. I now have a broken hand which isn't going to help Jonah nor will me being in pain stop his.

This was a lesson, a hard learnt one. But it taught me to think then act, rather than act in the heat of the moment when emotions are running high.

You can learn to control your emotions, you need to stop and think, assess the situation and decide on the best response.

You need to keep asking yourself questions until you become familiar with your emotions.

Break it down until you know them inside out.

You need to expose them and yourself to the world, you need to know what each emotion feels like. Don't confuse them.

Feel fear, anger etc...

Know the difference and how you deal with and control each one.

Never hold them in or repress your emotions. They build and fester and come out in a different way, a worse way. But at the same time don't let them run riot and be all over the place.

There's a time and place and always act your age, your emotion response changes as you mature.

Finally, never become complacent about your emotions, never say "I don't have emotions"

We all have emotions, even the toughest bastards do. They've just learnt and have worked hard to control them.

No matter who you are you can control your emotions, you don't need to be a hardened war veteran to do so.

Emotions are like waves, constantly flowing, the good and the bad. Ride them out but be in control.

Have control over your actions, reactions and words. Some shit you can't always control but you can control how you react to it.

Don't dwell, allowing a problem or situation to dominate your mind is a quick way to lose resilience. Be strong and focus on what is within control and act as soon as possible.

Regulating your emotions is pivotal.

Anger - pause and think clearly, respond rationally. The greatest remedy for anger is delay.

Overwhelmed - write what you need to do, focus on getting the smaller tasks done first. The ones that take 5 minutes are easy ones to get ticked off. Focus on one task at a time.

Insecure - appreciate and accept yourself, warts and all. You are more than you give yourself credit for.

Rejected - it's rubbish, but suck it up, we all face rejection at some point. Don't let it consume you, rejection is redirection.

Discouraged - be kind, remind yourself of why you are trying and what the end goal is. Use this as your strength.

Anxious - focus on the present and take deep breaths to regulate your breathing.

One of the best ways to regulate breathing is the box breathing method, used by special forces operatives to regulate breathing and become calmer and think more clearly. Box breathing is pretty simple when put into practice:

Breathe in for 4 seconds

Hold for 4 seconds

Breathe out for 4 seconds

Hold for 4 seconds

Repeat

Control your words, think before you speak. Engage brain before mouth.

Remember the rule of 5:

If someone can't change something in 5 minutes don't point it out, for example scars, stretch marks, skin problems and so on. If someone has food in their teeth point it out, it can be changed and remedied quickly. We have two eyes, two ears and a single mouth for a reason.

Fight it, or accept it.

Fear it, or control it.

Pain

We all feel pain, we just have different thresholds.

You don't need to be some man mountain or absolutely stacked to not feel pain. I've seen the smallest of people handle pain better than someone built like a brick shit house. On this occasion, size doesn't matter.

We've all seen people act hard and say they don't feel pain···bollocks. Everyone feels pain, whether emotionally or physically.

To truly understand pain, you need to understand your body and how pain affects it. You need know and understand how your body responds to pain and discomfort, the more you know and understand this the more control you will have.

You need to learn to embrace and accept pain and discomfort, the more you do this the more accepting you and your body will become.

Become comfortable being uncomfortable.

The more you put your mind and body in the hurt locker the better you become at accepting and embracing pain.

It's a mental and physical battle.

Never neglect your mind when it comes to dealing with and overcoming pain.

Your body will give up long before your mind, but if you have a weak mind you'll never get anywhere. It's your mind that will keep you going. If at the first sight of pain your mind gives up no matter how big or strong you are, you will not get anywhere.

Both your mind and body go hand in hand, so use them both. Both will help each other out. You can't rely on just one element to get you through.

Share the burden between the two, if one is flagging use the other to help with the load.

If you know you've got something physically and it can give your mind a bit of a break, do it. Your mind will thank you for it down the line.

Learn to use both your mind and body together to fight and deal with pain. Learn to know when you need more mind power or more body power.

Show up on the toughest days, we often have days where we feel absolute dog shit. But, showing up on those days often turn out to be the most important. Proving to yourself you can turn up on the tough days builds mental strength and resilience. I'm not saying turn up if feeling absolutely honking, you need to listen to your body.

Pain is temporary, it doesn't last forever.

Humour is key to dealing with pain and other multiple situations in life, I've used it many times to get me through situations. The Royal Marine Commandos embody this outlook. One of the Commando spirits is "cheerfulness in the face of adversity". Make humour the heart of morale. Pretty much, if things go tits up and there's not much you can do, just laugh, make a joke, it will help you and others around you. Learn to take the piss out of yourself and not take yourself too seriously all the time.

Pain is only French for bread.

Pain is real.

But so is hope.

No

Stand up for yourself.

No one else is going to do it for you, if you don't stand up for yourself no one will respect you.

Saying no doesn't need to be confrontational. Many of us hate confrontation, and just say what we think the other person wants to hear. We just nod and go along with it even though it's not what we actually want. We just want to please others, even though it could be at the expense of our own happiness.

Being confrontational doesn't need to be aggressive, don't attack the individual or become defensive. Talk to them and approach it like an adult, don't throw your toys out the pram like a child, this won't help your case. Let them know you have a problem and ask them to help you with it.

I used to love confrontation, and I'd go looking for it. I'd even say I'd thrive under it. I've learnt that you're more likely to get what you want from the situation if you meet the person halfway rather than being aggressive which doesn't help anyone.

How you say it and how you do it is everything and it's only down to you to put it across correctly and in the best possible manor.

You are only responsible for this, not how someone reacts to it. You can be as nice and considerate as possible, but some people just don't like to hear the truth or something they don't like the sound of. If they get upset or don't like it, tough. That's their decision, not yours.

Don't be scared of hurting someone's feelings. If something needs to be said, it needs to be said.

Violence isn't the answer, you're not in a war zone fighting for your life.

There's always a way around it without using violence. Do what you can to de-escalate the situation, it may even be walking away or not being too proud to apologise.

Saying no isn't weakness, it's actually looking after yourself and putting yourself first. If you do your best to put across your point and opinion in the best possible way that's all you can do. You can't help the reaction of the other person.

Just be an adult about it.

Part II
Habits

Habits

These are the daily things we do that can make or break you. Incorporating healthy habits into your routine will upgrade your life.

We are by nature creatures of habit. 45% of our reported activities in a given day are habitual, performed automatically without much thought.

Nearly half our actions each day are automatic.

Don't get me wrong, adding a new habit or subtracting a bad one is great. But think bigger. How about we take back control of half of what we will do for the rest of our lives.

Because habits occur outside the spectrum of thought we are inherently incapable of knowing how prevalent and influential they really are.

My own belief is that habits are not only more important than we *do* imagine, but more important than we *can* imagine.

Habits are the essential foundation for any productivity practice. The appearance of superhuman levels of self-discipline is simply a collection of strong habits, carefully cultivated over time.

Overnight success is a myth.

For life changing results, use discipline to build habits.

Discipline is the bridge between your goals and accomplishments.

First we build habits,

Then they build us.

Habit Creation

Simply put, triggers make a habit. Without a trigger we don't get a habit.

A trigger can be anything in our environment which our brains associate with a habit.

The factors such as where we are, who we are with and what we are doing, just so happen to have a powerful and invisible effect upon our behavior.

Every time a trigger precedes a habit, our brains strengthen the association between a habit and its trigger.

As an association between a habit and a trigger increases, the habit becomes more and more ingrained until we can perform our habits on full auto-pilot mode. As the trigger and habit association strengthens, the habit becomes more automatic. They become routine.

Over time it will be easier and easier to stick to the new habit.

No Trigger = No Habit.

Triggers are quite easy to recognise and create once you understand them fully.

The best triggers are all; Specific, Consistent, Automatic, Unavoidable.

Specific. The instructions are clear, leaving no room for interpretation.

Consistent. Happening every single day with a reliable frequency.

Automatic. The trigger happens on its own without any ongoing effort.

Unavoidable. You cannot do anything to avoid encountering the trigger.

There are a few categories of triggers.

Preceding event – it is important to realise that there are hundreds of pre-existing triggers already happening throughout your day. Every morning we get out of bed, get dressed, eat breakfast, brush our teeth, and arrive at our desk. Each of these preceding events represents an opportunity to stack on a new productive habit.

Many existing habits are an automatic response to something else that is happening in your life.

The list of potential triggers is endless, so experiment to learn what works best for you.

Time – our biological clocks make time a powerful trigger. We wake up, go to work, and eat our meals at similar times each day. Time can be very useful with habit building because it leaves no room for ambiguity and has a recurring predictability. 09:15 happens at the same time every day. The trouble is that we are not reliable timekeepers, actually we are shit and this is why it's very easy to lose track of time.

This is why we create automatic digital reminders for ourselves such as an alarm, a calendar event, or an app notification. Whatever works.

Location - location is a powerful driver of automatic habits. In many cases, our behaviour is simply a product of our surroundings. Putting ourselves in a supportive environment is the most important action we can take to ensure that we stick to our good habits. All of our familiar locations have habits, good and bad, already associated with them.

I find it handy to place the tools necessary for completing a habit in certain spaces. That way, there is no chance you miss seeing them. By placing them in obvious locations I remember my commitment to completing the habit. To utilise the location, I maintain strong mental contexts by having separate places in my house or surroundings for creative work, client-facing work, socialising and relaxation. Whenever you get stuck you can hit the reset button by moving to a new environment.

By shifting my location, I can shift my mindset.

Other people - besides genetics, peers are the primary predictors of our personalities and behavior.

If your habits aren't so great your friends' habits probably aren't so great either.

You are the average of the five people you surround yourself with.

This is a quote that is often repeated but rarely applied. Friends will reinforce and encourage the behaviours that they value and sabotage, usually unconsciously, the behaviours which they don't value. Simply put, spend more time around the people who embody the traits you want to create in yourself.

The two-day rule - don't let yourself take more than 1 day off when trying to forge a new habit. You need to follow through for at least 30 days. This rule allows you to take a break and avoid burnout while also ensuring you're staying on track and still working towards building your new habit.

Do it twice - Repetition

Do it a few times - Behavior

Do it over multiple months - Habit

Do it for a year - Routine

It's not what you do once in a while that shapes our lives, it's what we constantly do.

Habit Breaking

Similarly, an understanding of triggers is essential for an ability to break old habits.

Our old habits are constantly being reinforced by their triggers. We tend to repeat what we previously did in a similar situation. If the trigger for an old habit never occurs, the habit loop is interrupted. Without repeated reinforcement the association between habit and trigger weakens through neglect. Therefore, if we can eliminate our exposure to triggers for old habits, we can eliminate the habits themselves.

Think of a habit that you are trying to break or would like to break.

What are the current triggers which might set the habit in motion?

How can you decrease the likelihood of these triggers?

Can you:

Reduce the frequency of the preceding event?

Replace your association at that time of day?

Avoid the triggering location or make the environment less tempting?

Reduce the effects from a negative emotional state?

Find someone to support you in breaking this habit?

Is there someone you should be distancing yourself from?

If you are having a hard time breaking a habit, you need to create a separation from your triggers. Examine the circumstances where the habit is broken. Try changing your environment or with whom you spend time. Plan alternative responses for when you are in that emotional state.

You get what you repeat.

Good

There are many different habits you can add into your life and track from daily to monthly.

The most common healthy habits are: Meditate, Exercise, Limit Alcohol, Wake up early, Read, Write in journal, Drink more water, Go to gym, Take a walk outside, Wake up on time, Make bed, No sweets, No smoking, Cold shower.

Plus, many more.

Good habits are vital for a healthy happy life. You don't need to go crazy with it. Be sensible.

You'll find one good habit will lead to another, drinking more water will lead to feeling better so you'll want to exercise more which will then lead to you sleeping better.

It takes just one habit to start the ball rolling.

The longer you keep up your good habits the more luck you attract. You aren't born lucky you make your own luck by practicing good healthy habits.

Simple habits such as saying thank you will get you far.

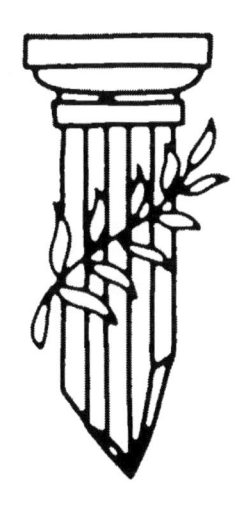

Bad

Emotions are common triggers for our bad habits. We eat, not because we are hungry, but because we are bored. We play mindless games or impulsively check social media, not because we enjoy them, but to distract us from our stress and anxiety. Which ultimately causes more anxiety.

I believe emotions are important signals from our subconscious that we should listen to rather than repress. We cannot change our bad habits until we diagnose the underlying causes of the emotions which are triggering them.

Bad habits vary from person to person, work out what yours are and work at giving them the boot.

Ugly

Ugly habits, no I'm not talking about picking your nose.

Ugly habits as I like to say are those habits that aren't the ones that are bad for your body or health, but the habits that are bad for your mental well-being and mind.

Habits like constant social media use, negative attitude, rudeness, plus many more.

These affect your mind and well-being, and this is why I call them ugly as you can do all you want to look great on the outside but if your habits are ugly then your ugly on the inside and this is what truly matters in the long run.

I've met plenty of people who look great and obviously look after themselves externally but seemed to have forgotten about the internal. You need to look after both. Don't have ugly habits.

Don't get sucked into repeating the same ugly habits that have an ugly effect on you and your well-being. Don't wake up and repeat the same old shit that fucks with your head and wellness.

If you struggle with anxiety then don't let the first thing you do be looking online, you'll see things that don't help you. Let's face it, we all follow people we shouldn't. If they don't add to your life, erase them.

Routine

Stack all of your habits together into routines.

In a routine each habit forms part of a structure which reinforces the other habits. This is particularly useful in the morning or before bed when energy and attention are lowest.

By completing the trigger action, you set the first routine habit in motion. This increases the chances of completing all of the habits in the routine.

For the best results make the first habit in the stack something you always do no matter what.

Having a routine filled with healthy habits is the key and aim. Once something becomes routine it's natural and rarely needs thinking about.

Having a morning routine and taking care of yourself for at least an hour before work will change your life. Give yourself this time to tune in with yourself before tuning in with anyone else.

Part III

Be Dangerous

Be Dangerous

I don't mean the I can kill you with one finger kind of dangerous, although it's a useful skill. But being dangerous in mind and lifestyle will make you one tough being.

People can look hard or even act hard, we've all seen it and experienced it. These people would soon shit themselves if put into a situation where being dangerous in mind and body is needed.

Anyone can punch or hit and think they are dangerous, and they are, to themselves. But being dangerous in mind, lifestyle and habit is different.

Go about it quietly, no need to shout about it. If you need to show you're dangerous then you aren't.

Beware the quietest man in the room.

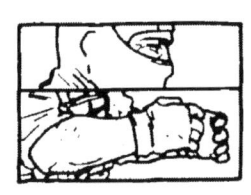

Workout

You can automatically look and feel better than 80% of the population by keeping fit and active.

When it comes to working out do your own thing, don't feel you need to do or follow these online trainers, they do what's best for them.

If you like running, run. If you'd rather spend time in the gym, do that. Just move and be active.

There isn't a right or wrong way, there's just a do it or don't.

It's pretty easy to be active. It's not bloody rocket science. You don't even need a gym membership; all you need is yourself to begin with.

Working out helps you both physically and mentally to become stronger and more resilient. If you get used to putting yourself in uncomfortable situations, then when an outside influence puts you in one you can deal with it much more easily.

Individuals who workout have a drive. They get up and they know at some point that day they will work out. It's this discipline and attitude that makes them dangerous.

If you can willingly get up and go and do something active, then you're winning. You beat all those who stay sat on their arses.

Each and every workout you do doesn't need to be amazing, some will be absolute dog shit I promise you. Don't get caught up on it or beat yourself up, as long as you're doing something.

Workouts still count too if you don't post them on social media, fucking mind blowing I know, but it's true. Train in private and let your results do the talking.

You don't need to do amazing things in your workouts, the best training programmes are pretty bloody boring.

Master the basics; Push, Pull, Carry and keep moving, it really is that simple. You don't need to do upside down 360 pull ups with a kettlebell between your legs, a bar balanced under your chin and a plate on each finger. It's just not needed and you're just asking for people to look at you.

Get yourself a training partner; when you have someone to train with you don't want to let them down and if you keep cancelling on them, they will get pissed off. Or get yourself a trainer to help to keep you on track. If you're paying for it, you won't want to waste your money.

When looking for a trainer go for one who will work on your mental fitness over your mentalis.

Train in silence and succeed in public.

Let them see the results, not the process.

Be the quiet one in the gym.

The best investment you can ever make is in your own mind and body.

Save elsewhere, spend lavishly on your own health and fitness.

Invest in health.

Health in wealth.

Pain of discipline,

Or pain of regret.

You decide.

Mean It

Do what you said you were going to do.
Accomplish your goals, people will listen to this.

If you say you're going to do something, bloody do it. Don't be full of empty words and shit. People will pay attention to you if you're a man or woman of their word.

Empty promises are the sign of a weak person, we all know people who say things like "yeah I'll do that, I'll say this" etc... we all know we will never see the day they will actually do it. Don't be this person.

If you want to say what you truly mean you don't need to be a twat about it. Give and receive input, give honest feedback and be open to receiving the same.

Bloody listen, we've got two ears and one mouth for a reason.

Stay in the moment of what you said you were going to do. And most importantly don't bloody quit.

At the end of the day people don't respect other people who are all talk and no action. Ultimately your word is your bond.

People will think twice about messing with you if you do what you say and act on your words.

Don't be full of empty promises, if you know you can't act on them don't make them.

Meaning what you say and do should show respect and receive respect from others, remember we earn respect, it isn't freely given.

This can be done in many ways:

Be the last to speak – this shows you listen and process the information.

Laugh at yourself – this shows you have a sense of humour and don't take things too seriously…time and a place remember.

Actions speak louder than words - a picture can show a thousand words, exactly the same goes for actions.

Be honest, say what you mean.

See the good in everything and everyone - everyone we meet and everything we do is a lesson. Don't judge a book by it's cover.

Respect - treat others how you wish to be treated.

Change yourself - we are either getting better or getting worse.

Help others when they ask for it and ask for help if you need it, don't be too proud.

Don't Give A F*ck

Probably the most important one of all, not giving a fuck is key. When you don't care or react to bullshit people get scared. When you don't respond people realise they have no control over you.

Opinions are like arseholes, everyone's got one. Most people who throw their opinion on you have no right, they don't know you, they don't know your story or where you've been or going. What they say or think has no bearing on you. Don't give them the time of day.

A prime example is the gym environment; many people are anxious of going into a gym because they are scared what others will think, they are scared people look at them and judge.

If someone does look at you in the gym and judges you it's their problem not yours, let them judge. If they have nothing better to do let them crack on. No one in a gym environment should be judged.

Let's be honest, most people in the gym are too wrapped up and self-involved with themselves to even notice anyone else in the gym, usually too busy taking selfies.

Note: mirrors in gyms are not for selfies, they are for checking your form.

Most young lads in gyms are full of piss, wind and protein powder so their opinions are void.

What I'm getting at is this, stop giving a fuck what people may or may not be looking at or judging. As soon as you do this you will have a lot more freedom and a huge weight of your shoulders.

If someone gives you shit, or they try to give you "banter" then just ignore it. If you don't give a response, then you've taken all power away from them.

Take the higher ground.

Most people want a response from you, if you do respond you're playing into their hands.

Care about what you should, family etc... but the opinions and views of the sheep have no right to even enter your head space.

The not giving a fuck attitude will put people off trying to mess with you, or believing they can walk over you, because they won't get the response they want from you.

Smile, laugh, walk away and don't give a fuck.

Create

Create solutions. Too many people complain - laugh in the faces of the complainers.

Life is full of complainers, every day we hear it, it's boring. If people spent the time they are complaining actually create and coming up with solutions, they wouldn't be in said situation in the first place.

Don't like something? Do something about it.

Grow through what you go through.

We can all complain, mostly about work.

Leaders create solutions, do you want to be the leader in your life, of course you do. You don't want to be the puppet.

Good leaders build the environment and structure around them and develop solutions for whatever comes their way.

They take the right path not the easy path.

If you want to be a problem solver and solution creator, make it simple. Don't create unnecessary stress for you and others.

Make the process simple.

Take full accountability for your actions. Only you can create solutions for your problems, don't rely on others to do it for you.

Want to progress in your career? Do this!

Companies want leaders and individuals to lead by example. Stop hiding behind others and come to the front.

Someone who creates solutions for their problems rather than complaining about them is a force to be reckoned with. No matter what you complain about, do something about it. Rather than filling someone else's head with this pointless shit, act.

Weak people constantly complain, strong people act and create solutions.

Stance

Posture, how you hold and portray yourself by how you stand is huge. People look and see our body language first; it is our first impression of people.

If you're standing looking like a sack of shit, then people notice this. Why should they expect anything from you? If you don't have pride in yourself to stand tall and not slouch then people won't respect you, why should they. You're not respecting yourself or portraying that you deserve respect.

How we stand when talking to people says a lot too, we can not say a word to someone but how we stand can say more than anything words ever can.
Standing with your arms crossed is like putting a wall up, it closes you off from who you're trying to connect with. Crossing your arms comes across as aggressive and portrays you've got no interest.

Hands in your pockets is just laziness and looks messy. There's no reason to stand with your hands

in your pockets. They aren't that heavy.
Body language while talking to others says a lot, if you're too busy standing scratching your arse or pulling out a wedgie it shows disrespect. You're concentrating more on yourself.

In the military you're taught to not scratch your face or wipe away sweat when conducting physical training. This is because, in the field when trying to be quiet and unseen moving to wipe away sweat or a bug will make a noise and compromise your position.

This is basic discipline. Have discipline and control over your body.

Eye contact is a huge element to this, if you're too busy looking round at random shit going on it shows no respect to those you're talking to. It also portrays that you have no trust in what you're saying and that you can't be trusted. If someone doesn't make eye-contact with me I find it odd. I'm not saying stare people out like a fucking psycho.

Giving your full attention, standing right, and eye contact, will tell others so much about you before you even open your mouth.
Stand tall, stand straight, have your hands behind your back, by your side or in front of you. Be welcoming to people with your posture.

Good posture shows pride, eye contact shows trust and confidence in what you're saying, those with pride and confidence are a force to be reckoned with.

Eyes are loud.

Part IV Wellness

Wellness

We all hear this word floating around. But what actually is wellness, what can it do for you and how can it aid you in developing a strong and resilient mind.

Wellness is a pretty modern term, but the roots and meaning are ancient. Think back to the stoics of ancient Greece and Rome. Even though these civilizations are long gone we can still learn a lot from them.

Put simply, wellness is a cocktail of intellectual, religious and medical movements. It is a pursuit of activities, choices and lifestyle choices that lead to a state of holistic health.

Holistic I hear you groan. I'm not saying ditch the clothes, go all natural and become a hippie, hugging trees and tie dying all your white shirts. But in ancient times they didn't have access to medicine like we do so everything they did was natural and more of the holistic approach.

Emotional

Be able to understand and cope with your feelings.

You need to be aware of, accept, and express your feelings. And, just as importantly, understand the feelings of others.

I'm not saying you need to be an absolute emotion sponge and soak up everything you or others feel. You need to decide what to let in and who to let in.

Showing and feeling emotion is good, it's human.

How you feel can affect your ability to carry out everyday activities, your relationships and your overall mental health and mindset.

A strong emotional wellness is the ability to successfully handle life's stresses and adapt to change and difficult times and situations.

Build resilience - building resilience will allow you to have fewer negative emotions. Learning healthy ways to cope and deal with situations can help you build resilience.

Reducing stress - easier said than done as there are people out there who just love to cause you stress. Short bursts of stress can give you a rush of energy. But prolonged or chronic stress isn't healthy. Learning healthy ways to cope with stress can also boost your resilience.

Sleep - sleep is paramount to emotional health and well-being. We often sacrifice sleep to get more into our day. But neglecting sleep will affect both our physical and mental health. Take steps to make sure you get regular decent sleep.

If needs be, nap.

Stop living on autopilot, floating around your day and life not having a scooby of what's going on around you. Be aware of what's going on, be mindful. Don't go through life like a zombie.

Loss - when we lose someone we care about, the world changes. It's shit, no one likes loss, but unfortunately, it's part of life. There is no right or wrong way to mourn. You must make sure you take care of yourself, talk to friends and be patient. As shit as loss is it is something we must learn to deal with.

Spiritual

Firstly, you don't need to become a witch or wizard to be spiritual. Having spiritual wellness is having a purpose and meaning in life, this includes your morals and ethics. It doesn't need to involve religious activities.

We all need a meaning in life and each of us will have a different answer to this.

Personal reflection:

What gives your life meaning and purpose?

What gives you hope?

Where do you find comfort?

Do you make time for relaxation?

Do your values guide your decisions and actions?

When practicing spiritual wellness, it's best to find something that suits you and your personality. You can meditate or participate in yoga. You can spend quiet time alone pondering. You could create a journal or simply spend time in nature (you don't need to hug trees, walking among them is absolutely fine!), walking by water is incredible for this.

Feel lonely when you're alone? This is because you have no purpose. Give yourself a purpose then it's a privilege to be alone and focus and get things done.

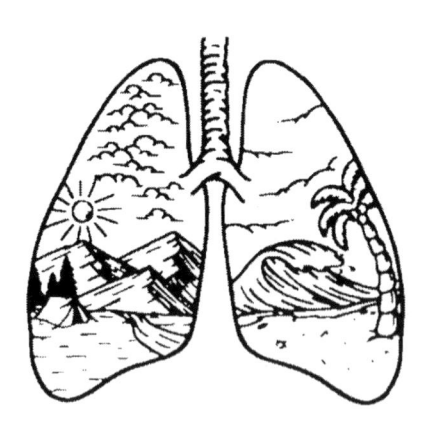

Intellectual

You don't need to be a A* student to be intellectual, I'm certainly not an A* student, the highest grades I got were C. This doesn't mean I'm not an intellectual, I just struggled at school, the generic teaching methods didn't work for me. I only really learnt when I was in the military because they knew people needed different methods and environments to learn in.

Becoming intellectual means striving towards a good mental health, continued intellectual growth and being creative.

This can be achieved pretty easily. You can continue learning, there is always something to learn no matter what job you're in. I am a health, fitness and lifestyle coach and am constantly learning. I need to be, as times and methods change. Never sit on your laurels when it comes to learning and never be too proud to say you need to learn something.

Keep up to date with social and political issues, you may think it's boring but everything we do involves this.

Read; magazines, books, newspapers are all good, and reading opens the mind and allows learning.

Being an intellectual doesn't mean Einstein. We all have our own intelligence, some of us are good at maths and English, others are more creative. No one is dumb or stupid, we all have intelligence in our own areas.

Read to save yourself from ignorance.

Write to save yourself from confusion.

Notice details no one else sees.

Social

The relationships we have and how we interact with others is our social well-being.

This involves building healthy, nurturing relationships and being supportive in the ones we have. Whether it be romantic, family or friends. All matter.

You need to make effort and make it a priority to keep in touch with those who are supportive. Whether they be family, friends or mentors.

We've all done it when getting into a relationship, we've dropped our friends then inevitably, when the relationship goes tits up, had to go crawling back. Often, we may find that it is our other half that stops us from seeing our friends. If this happens, it's toxic. We need friends and company outside of our relationships, keep it fresh.

Join a club or organization, or even volunteer. This will develop bonds and friendships. Joining a gym will do this too, you could meet people who you can train with.

By all means be social and go to social events, drink if you want to drink. But don't live to drink or live for the weekend. There are 7 days in a week, not 2. If you're living for 2 days, you'll end up wasting and wishing away the other 5.

You can still be social during the week. If you feel you can only be social with a drink in hand, sort it out.

Being social is great but remember not to let outside influences affect you. People only become disappointed in you when they can't manipulate you. Don't want to go out? Fine, don't. It's your choice.

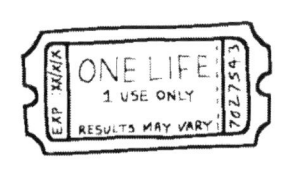

We often make the most foolish choices when we are lonely. Learn how to be happy alone, your life will sort itself out.

I find it sad when people say they hate being alone and don't like their own company. To me this says that they don't like themselves. If you don't like someone or think they are a twat you don't hang out with them, simple. They are a sponge. Love you time.

Making yourself fit in and following the crowd will make you miserable. Be yourself and if people don't want to hang with you fuck them, but keep the ones who stick around close.

Associate only with people who improve you.

Physical

Physical wellness is all about doing what you can to help strengthen and care for your body.

Maintaining physical wellness allows you to maintain a quality of life that allows you to get the most out of your daily activities without fatigue or creating undue physical stress.

You need to find time to move your body. Even just 30 minutes a day is enough, it can be broken down however you wish, 3 x 10 minutes.

Use stairs when you can, don't be lazy. Any little activity helps. Walking or cycling to work or the shops instead of driving. With the price of fuel being as it is walking or cycling should be tempting.

Learn to listen to your body; if you're feeling ill, rest. Resting isn't quitting. Have a day or two off to allow your body to recover, it will thank you for it in the long run. We can have up to 2 weeks off without doing any lasting damage to our bodies.

There are plenty of other habits and lifestyle choices we can perform to increase our physical wellness, these range from sleep, nutrition, hydration, exercise.

Working on these will improve all round well-being.

Tasks such as hydration are pretty easy to nail, get yourself a big water bottle and get through it. You want a minimum of 2 litres per day, more if you're active.

Eating right is pretty much common sense, we all know takeaways are full of saturated fats and general badness and we all know what foods are less than ideal and what foods are better for us.

I don't believe any food is bad, nor should food ever be called bad or a sin. Only the amount or portion size is bad for us.

Like chocolate? Eat it. I love a pastry and cheesecake, so I bloody well eat them. No, I don't have them for breakfast that often. But it's all in moderation. If you work out hard and you're active then eat more, as you're using up these calories.

There are no bad foods, just calories and bad *amounts* of food (whether it be too much or too little). Every food and drink have calories, watch out for these.

100 calories of chocolate are the same as 100 calories of salad.

It's your decision.

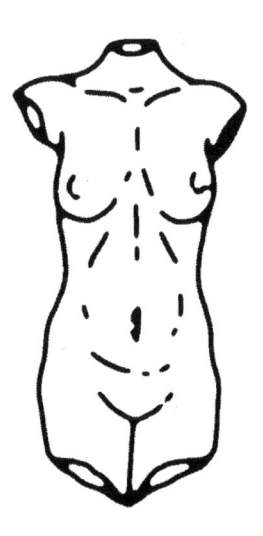

Career

Wellness in your career can be defined as engaging in work that provides personal satisfaction and enrichment that's consistent with your values, goals and lifestyle.

We all need and should have occupational wellness.

We need to be motivated and interested in our work. Yes, sometimes we will have to do boring mundane tasks, that's life. We still need to wash our clothes and iron them. Boring but necessary.

Feeling inspired and challenged is vital. Again, sometimes we want an easy day, but we don't want an easy life. Nothing in life worth having is easy. So, work for it and work bloody hard for it.

Don't settle, keep motivated and work hard towards what you want.

A work life balance is important, don't live to work. Find something you enjoy and what you're good at and make it your passion and job.

Establishing a healthy work life balance is key to doing what you love. This can be achieved in a multitude of ways.

Create a routine, make sure you give yourself time for breaks, eat, stretch your legs.

Turn off, get away from the screen, give your eyes a rest and don't let work take time away from you time or family time.

Change clothes, don't spend all the time in your work clothes. Separate work and you time.

Enjoy what you do and do what you enjoy.

Yes, easier said than done. But, if you're stuck in a job you detest, do something about it.

I'm not saying walk out with your middle finger up to your boss shouting fuck you and fuck this place. We've all been there where we've wanted to do this.

Take your time, start a side hustle, let your job pay for that then in time you can go and do what you love.

Some of us work better in companies and don't want to be our own boss, that's fine. Find a company that have the same ideas, goals and beliefs as you.

We spend most of our time at work, make it a happy enjoyable place to be.

Not all hustle is loud.

Part V
EverydayCombat

EverydayCombat

The title of this book, EverydayCombat is a phrase I've come up with myself.

It sums up everything covered in this book.

It's a combination of everything from mental fitness to habits and the way you decide to live your life.

We need to practice and perform all these things every day to be the healthiest and happiest we possibly can.

No, it's not easy, but nothing worth having ever is. And this is where the combat comes in, for none of these tasks are easy to achieve. It takes courage, dedication and hard work to achieve all this and put yourself in uncomfortable situations. We go into combat with ourselves each and every day. Leading a healthy, happy lifestyle and becoming strong and resilient in mind and body is an everyday combat.

Pace

This is all a lot to take in. Some traits you may already have, but others will need work.

You need to attack this at your own pace, don't overwhelm yourself with trying to take on everything in one go.

Break it down into more manageable chunks, spend a week or two on each different habit or skill you want to take on and master.

The longer something takes to settle in and become habit or routine the longer it will last.

You need to nurture these habits and work hard on them, you need to practice them every day.

Enjoy a slower pace to life, living at a more leisurely pace, taking stock and savoring the simple things in life. Being more leisurely also means an increased mindfulness of the impact of our actions on us, others and the planet.

This also allows us to have an increased awareness of our actions on our lives and health. This automatically encourages us to slow down a little and think.

Live fast, die young, this is a questionable motto. No one really wants to die young; we all want a full life. If you enjoy extreme sports, fine. Embrace speed, enjoy it. But don't rush your life and the habits. If you go all in and don't pace yourself, you'll speed through what should take weeks, month possibly years.

Treat life like a game of chess; think, process and move.

Enjoy the process, take it all in.

Embrace

Embrace the process and the changes the good changes it will make to your life.

You need to be willing to embrace change for this to work and to actually make a difference.

We as humans are designed for change, it's how we adapt and overcome. If we never change, we'd have never evolved to where we are now.

Change is good and is needed.

Think back in your life, the times things changed and the good that has come of it. Maybe at the time you were shitting it saying you don't like change and don't want to accept it.

Embracing ourselves is important and it involves a lot, it provides us with self-confidence, self-worth and in general we feel more positive.

There will be times of change that haven't been good, that's life. But you have to embrace it, if it's in your power then do something about it, if it isn't then accept it. Heal and shift.

Make peace with it.

Have courage to change.

Pressure

We all put ourselves under pressure, which then brings on stress and multiple other issues which will affect us.

We also shouldn't let others put pressure on us. Whether it be family, friends or at work.

We have full control over the pressure we put ourselves under. Yes, they say diamonds were formed under pressure, and wine is formed from grapes being crushed, but we are not bloody diamonds or grapes.

When it comes to pressure it can make things overwhelming for us. As soon as this happens it puts us off and we think, fuck it, won't bother.

In some aspects pressure is good. Some individuals can thrive under it. But they only thrive in those situations because of training and putting themselves in the situation time and time again. The more you repeat something, or something happens to you, you learn to cope with it and deal with the situation.

You are your master. You decide the amount of pressure you want to put yourself under.

The more reasons we have to do something, the more reasons we have not to do it.

Keep it simple and lower the pressure on yourself.

Process

It's a long one, accept it.

Pace it and embrace it.

Everyone has the same 24 hours in each day, lack of time isn't the problem. If you want a better, healthier, happier life, then just invest your time more intelligently. We process each day and task differently, learn to process your day right.

Long the road may be and full of ups and downs, the destination is worth it.

The main thing is you embrace it, each and every step, no matter how little it may feel. Each little step is leading you to taking a huge leap in improving your life and the lives of those around you.

Everything we do in life has a process, making a cup of tea, running a bath, everything. These processes become habitual and routine. You need to make the other habits, lifestyle choices and movements this also.

Trust in the process and you will succeed, don't give up, stick it out.

Learn to prioritise the long term over the short-term pleasure.

Thrive

Your mission and aim in life shouldn't be just to merely survive, but to thrive. And to do this with:

Passion, Compassion, Humor and Style

There are many ways you can thrive in life; many have already been covered throughout this book already. The little habits you repeat each day will help you to thrive and live the life you deserve. When you wake up and thrive in all you do throughout the day it becomes natural, and you will thrive at life.

Once you thrive in life the possibilities are endless.

To thrive is pretty simple in reality, taking care of your mind, body and spirit will set you well on your way.

Simple things like trying something new or acting like a kid will help.

Simply put, thriving is when you develop, succeed or master something.

Put in even simpler terms it is feeling good about life and yourself and being good at something.

T - thankful

H - hopeful

R - resting

I - inspiring

V - victorious

E - eternally thriving

Strive

To strive means you make great efforts to achieve or obtain something. To strive in life and for excellence you need to want to thrive,

Firstly, striving for excellence isn't the same as perfection. Perfectionism is a personal standard which we hold ourselves to, and if being completely honest it's unattainable. We can spend hours working out the tiny details. I've done that with this book, but I had to put a line under it at some point, I just kept criticising it.

Perfectionists fear failure and, as mentioned, failure is the greatest of life lessons.

Now, striving is the opposite. Strive for you, be who you want to be.

Know your true self and your strengths and weaknesses.

Have pride in yourself and what you've done.

Share your knowledge and talents with people who want to listen and learn.

Believe in yourself. Have faith in you and your abilities.

Honour you and your needs. Make you and them a priority.

These along with other items mentioned will help you.

Surely, healthy striving is better than worrying.

Choose happiness.

Choose excellence

Choose you

Succeed

Succeed, that's all we want to do, no matter what it is. But many of us don't actually succeed at life. We all see success differently, but no matter how you see it you need to make your life a success. This doesn't mean be the wealthiest person, have the best belongings or be the strongest, but to succeed at living the happiest, healthiest most fulfilling life you can. This is success.

You can achieve a successful life by combining all areas discussed within this book. These are the main principles of success.

Remember success isn't easy, it's a bumpy road and has its ups and downs. If you expect it to be a straight upward line to success, you're kidding yourself.

To succeed you need to practice everything mentioned in this book. It will take a while and it won't be smooth. Ride it out and you and your life will be a success.

The harder the journey, the stronger you become.

End Notes

Take-aways

There is a lot to take away from this book, a lot.

But, with everything covered and mentioned, it will give you the tools and advice to create the lifestyle needed to forge a happy, healthy mind and body.

As mentioned throughout, take one step at a time, take your time. There is no rush. Leading a happy, healthy lifestyle and having a strong, resilient mind is a long journey and it should take time as it needs to be performed every day for the rest of your life.

Use this book to dive in and out of. You will come across situations in your life where you will go, what the fuck do I do now, how do I deal with this dickhead, I've fucked up, and so on.

This book will help you deal with these situations in the best way possible without putting yourself in the firing line or putting your mental well-being at risk.

Utilising this book to its full potential will help you become a dangerous human where nothing and no one can fuck with you. By using the power of the mind.

Once you realise how quickly the year passes, and how you have less time than you thought, you naturally acquire a sense of urgency.

Later = Never

Do it now

No one will do this for you, nor can they. It's all up to you. Build a strong resilient mind that's unsinkable and unflappable and everything else will follow.

Use this book, use others, use anything that helps you achieve this.

Thrive, Strive, Succeed

No risk,

No story.

Everyday Combat

Printed in Poland
by Amazon Fulfillment
Poland Sp. z o.o., Wrocław
22 August 2022

12df7658-1a7d-4d8f-83df-70bc8c87bb2aR01